PAST & PRESENT

DOWNTOWN PROVIDENCE

OPPOSITE: The Industrial Trust Building in Exchange Place, overlooking Depot Park, became the central focus of Downtown Providence in 1928 because it was the tallest building in Rhode Island at that time. This Art Deco–style structure was built because of the bank's need for more office space due to its large business interests in the New England area. (Author's collection.)

DOWNTOWN PROVIDENCE

Louis Azar II

I would like to dedicate this book to my wife, Patricia.

Library of Congress Control Number: 2021948993

Published by Arcadia Publishing
Charleston, South Carolina

Printed in the United States of America

For all general information, please contact Arcadia Publishing:
Telephone 843-853-2070
Fax 843-853-0044
E-mail sales@arcadiapublishing.com
For customer service and orders:
Toll-Free 1-888-313-2665

Visit us on the Internet at www.arcadiapublishing.com

ON THE FRONT COVER: Market Square was a political and commercial center for the colonial settlement of Providence and was permanently established with the construction of the Market House, built in 1773. Market Square was ideally located for local merchants and maritime trade because of the high pedestrian traffic in this area and its proximity to the local wharves. (Past, courtesy of Providence Public Library. Identifier: VM013_WC0859. This image was cropped for publication; present, author's collection.)

ON THE BACK COVER: This view of Exchange Street in 1920 is looking south toward the intersection of Westminster and Weybosset Streets from Exchange Place, now Kennedy Plaza. This Downtown Providence area was significant in the history of the city because it was and still is part of the financial district. This is where there were banks and professional offices such as the Banigan Building, Industrial Trust Building, Exchange Bank, and Turks Head Building. (Courtesy of Providence Public Library, Rhode Island Photograph Collection. Identifier: VM013_WC1307. This image was cropped for publication.)

CONTENTS

ACKNOWLEDGMENTS

This is to thank the many people that have helped me make this book possible. First, I would like to recognize the vintage postcard collectors across the United States and Canada from whom I purchased many of the unique postcards used in this book. Also, I would like to acknowledge the Rhode Island Historical Society and their research staff for the detailed information given to me, which helped me understand the history of Downtown Providence. In addition, a special thank-you to Providence Public Library for contributing the wonderful black and white photographs from their collection and to their great staff who helped me navigate their wonderful digital library. I would like to recognize the concise information from the historians and their publications noted in the bibliography, which helped me to clearly understand how Providence developed into the magnificent city it is today. I would like to show gratitude to the many professors of Providence College Graduate School of History and their staff who helped me appreciate the study of historical information that educated me on how to formulate and understand the past through research and documentation. Furthermore, I would like to thank Arcadia Publishing and their wonderful staff who helped me with the process of editing and publishing a photographic history of Downtown Providence.

INTRODUCTION

Downtown Providence, Rhode Island, has a magnificent collection of historic buildings that were built for shopping and financial services. The early retail businesses of Downtown Providence date as far back as 1773 in the Market Square area. The downtown area experienced unprecedented economic growth during its heyday between 1866 and 1928. These century-old buildings continue to fit in with the new economy of the 21st century. Each building had its own unique business history regarding how it was instrumental in the expansion of Providence's economy. Some examples of the buildings and businesses that were key to the economy of downtown are Shepard's Department Store, Gladding's dry goods store, the Outlet Company Store, and Tilden-Thurber. In addition to the retail businesses in the downtown area, there were financial service businesses and their buildings. These professional and bank buildings include the Turks Head Building, Industrial Trust Building, Banigan Building, and the Union Trust Building, to name a few. Many of these early businesses and the proprietors who ran them became the business innovators and civic leaders that helped direct the unprecedented modernization of the retail and financial markets in Providence.

The growth of Rhode Island's commercial sector was rapid in the downtown area beginning in 1866 with the Boston Store, the city's first retail department store. Growth continued with the influx of money from investors that accelerated the construction of more modern and larger buildings that changed the city's skyline with the introduction of the skyscraper. The buildings of the past in this great city, some forever gone, tell the fascinating story of Downtown Providence's wonderful history.

The first commercial and civic center in Providence was Market Square, established in 1773 with the construction of the Market House and the forerunner to Exchange Place. Market Square was the nucleus for municipal, financial, and retail business in the area because of its proximity to the wharves and Narragansett Bay through the Providence River. Many of the buildings in this area included small-sized office and retail buildings and warehouses. Market Square during its inception revolved around a maritime economy.

The focus of downtown's commercial center shifted in 1848 from Market Square in the east to the western lands of the city that included Exchange Place, Westminster Street, and Weybosset Street. The focus switched to the west because farther east toward College Hill was too congested with older buildings, and the topography was too steep. The new vision for the expansion of the downtown west from Market Square became a unified plan designed by civic leaders who considered a more uniform street pattern to allow the expansion of commercial interests and a pedestrian friendly area in the downtown. This plan eventually brought the main streets surrounding Exchange Place together with Westminster Street, Weybosset Street, and Dorrance Street. Other important thoroughfares that become integral to the downtown flow of commerce and pedestrian traffic are Fulton Street, Exchange Terrace, Exchange Street, and the many other roads west of the Providence River to Cathedral Square.

The idea to switch business focus from Market Square began as early as 1828 when the Arcade was built with the distinction of having two unique entrances, one on Weybosset Street and the other on

Westminster Street. This iconic Greek Revival structure was the first indoor shopping mall in the country and is still in use today. Other historic business buildings that are still being used today include the Banigan Building, Turks Head Building, Union Trust Building, Hospital Trust Building, and the currently vacant Industrial Trust Building. These buildings, deemed skyscrapers when built, were some of the tallest structures in New England in the 1930s. Market conditions deteriorated in Providence and across the United States because of the stock market crash of 1929, stopping any large-scale building projects at that time. Many of these early-20th-century buildings are still being used today as financial and professional office and retail buildings. In addition, many other century-old structures are being converted today to loft-style apartments by real estate investors and by local colleges and universities for dormitories and libraries.

The reasons Downtown Providence became an economic center were the railroad, immigration, urbanization, technology, a skilled workforce, industrialization, and state, municipal, and private capital investments. Of all these reasons, the one that made Downtown Providence expand in many areas was the influx of the immigrant population. Between 1840 and 1930, the city's population grew from 23,171 to 252,981. Another decisive reason for the city's capital growth was because it had a modern industrial infrastructure that had been built during the Civil War, which ended in 1865. In the years following the war, Providence had a large capacity to produce goods efficiently, so it switched to a consumer-based economy from a wartime one. This merging of many new factors inspired the expansion and success of downtown's financial and retail districts throughout its existence.

Today, downtown's financial district still has the most financial services facilities in Rhode Island. The city has an important relationship with the colleges and universities in the state, and many of the schools have bought and rehabilitated older buildings for educational use, which has given new life to the city's economy. The interesting architecture in Downtown Providence shows a variety of commercial and municipal structures not very often seen in 21st-century cities. This is unique because many of the buildings are within walking distance of one another, making it a great city to visit for a day or to reside in. The future of the city will be developed through a new plan called the Capital City Project.

Thankfully, many buildings of Downtown Providence were saved by city and state leaders over the years from demolition. Providence has survived over the decades to continue its vital role as the leading business area in the state. Today, the continued collaboration of state and local government is very important to the survival of the historic buildings of Downtown Providence. Though some historic buildings have been lost because of age, fire, or business expansion, the city and business leaders of today have an acute understanding that it is important to preserve the downtown's architecture of the past so future generations can appreciate it.

CHAPTER 1

COLONIAL PROVIDENCE AND MARKET SQUARE

RKET SQUARE, LOOKING EAST, PROVIDENCE, R. I.

Market Square was within the Township of Providence and was the center of political power in 1773. This area on the eastern side of Providence was developed because the area to the west was muddy and less suitable for commercial use. The Market House in the center of this image was refurbished in 1865, and in 1866 was rebranded the City Building. (Author's collection.)

The Board of Trade Building, known as the Market House (shown on the right), was erected in 1773 at the bottom of College Street; it was used for civic gatherings and municipal offices. This was where many retailers would gather at the open-air markets to sell their meats, poultry, and produce from carts and horse-drawn wagons. To the left of the Market House are several blocks of retail and office buildings. (Both, author's collection.)

A917 - Board of Trade Building, Market Square, Providence, R. I.

COLONIAL PROVIDENCE AND MARKET SQUARE

These images shows the northeast section of Market Square at the bottom of North and South Main Streets in 1900 and illustrate the size of the buildings that were typically found in this commercial area. Some of the buildings in this block included the Roger Williams Bank Building (1823–1912), the Manufacturers Hotel (1750– 1850), and the What Cheer Block (1850–1955). This historic section was the commercial center of Providence and eventually faded out when the city expanded west to Exchange Place, Westminster Street, and Weybosset Street. (Both, author's collection.)

This view of Market Square shows the amount of space the municipal government allowed for the fruit peddlers who began selling here in 1773. The Weybosset Street Bridge section in this area was designated for vendors because of its proximity to storage buildings nearby. Eventually, these vendors formed a more permanent business in 1927 by incorporating the Providence Terminal Produce Market. (Both, author's collection.)

This is a westerly view of the Hospital Trust Building and the Federal Building in the eastern area of Market Square. This modernization of the downtown with the influx of more institutional businesses and government buildings would eventually overshadow the open market vendor-style businesses for larger business models. Beginning in 1918, the peddlers were moved indoors closer to Union Station, which helped relieve traffic congestion in this area for further modernization. (Both, author's collection.)

THE HOSPITAL TRUST BUILDING AND POST OFFICE, PROVIDENCE, R. I.

Rhode Island School of Design (RISD) was established in 1877, and this image shows the Waterman Street Building, which was within walking distance of Market Square and Downtown Providence. This prestigious school was envisioned by a prominent group of women led by Helen Adelia Rowe Metcalf. The school helped train artists in the skills needed to be the builders and designers of the future. Today, RISD is still one of the top schools in the country. (Both, author's collection.)

ovidence, R.I. Market Square, showing Old Car Station.

In the center of this vintage postcard is the "Old Car Station." The official name of this one-story building was the Union Station, and it was built in 1867. This conveniently located shelter was in a very high-traffic area of Market Square. It allowed pedestrians to take one of the many trolley cars to numerous destinations in Rhode Island, Connecticut, and Massachusetts. (Both, author's collection.)

COLONIAL PROVIDENCE AND MARKET SQUARE

2178—Market Square, Providence, R. I.

Souvenir Post Card Co., New York and Berlin

The early years of Providence's retail and financial businesses revolved around a maritime economy. Market Square extended to South Water Street and Dyer Street, as seen in this postcard. This historical wharf area was Providence's shipping center in 1773 because of its proximity to downtown. This area also included banks and retail stores. The area started to fade with the construction of Exchange Place in 1848. (Both, author's collection.)

Providence Harbor was a major factor in the growth of Downtown Providence in the early 1800s and 1900s. This early image of the harbor showing ferries, ships, and warehouses loading and unloading cargo illustrates how vital this area was to downtown. Looking to the right are the wharves just west of the Crawford Street Bridge on Dyer Street, and on the left is South Water Street. (Both, author's collection.)

G 872   River Boats at Crawford Street Bridge, Providence, R. I.

This bird's-eye view of Canal Street and Market Square shows how busy the area was between 1773 and 1848. Canal Street was one of the oldest streets in the downtown and was situated along the Providence canal. This waterway was used for the transport of goods from the nearby wharves. To the left are the many businesses that occupied this area. (Both, author's collection.)

Birds Eye View of Canal St. and Market Sq. Providence, R. I.

COLONIAL PROVIDENCE AND MARKET SQUARE

Steamships were an important way to travel around New England, because the region had many waterways. This view of the downtown wharves shows several ships at dock loading and unloading passengers and cargo. One of the first steamboat businesses out of Providence was owned by Richard Borden in 1827; the line went from Fall River to Providence. (Both, author's collection.)

Peoples Savings Bank was founded in 1857 and constructed this building on 27 North Main Street in 1913 near Market Square, just behind the Board of Trade Building. Although this bank was built during the time of economic growth in Downtown Providence, it was minuscule compared to the Banigan Building, Providence's first skyscraper. This unique bank building is now owned by RISD. (Both, author's collection.)

This image of Market Square looking north shows the Banigan Building at left and the Rhode Island State House in the center background. There is quite a size difference between the older buildings and the newly designed Banigan Building. The foreground shows the open-air market with peddlers selling their products. This street scene was typical in the Market Square area in the 1890s. Many of these older buildings have been replaced by newer ones. (Both, author's collection.)

Morning Scene, Market Square, Providence, R. I.

Crawford Street Bridge, built around 1870 and rebuilt in 1930, was in Market Square downtown and was the primary throughway that connected Dyer and South Water Streets. This bridge was used by many commuters and businesses to gain access to the wharves and to easily reach the central downtown markets from the east side. (Both, author's collection.)

COLONIAL PROVIDENCE AND MARKET SQUARE

The Providence River waterfront was the gateway to the city for all maritime shipping. The river was used to transport commodities to the city such as lumber, coal, oil, and dry goods. It was dredged and widened to accommodate larger ships by 1853. Large warehouse facilities, such as the Providence Coal Company, were built on the wharves to store these products as well as other dry goods for the growing city. (Both, author's collection.)

College Hill was and still is a popular section of downtown located on College Street. The two main roads that connect this street are South and North Main Streets. This area was original to Market Square. The steep hill to the east made expansion of this area to more commuter traffic impossible. Trollies ascending the hill needed a form of counter weighting to negotiate the climb. (Both, author's collection.)

College Hill, Providence, R.I. Dear Ada,

COLONIAL PROVIDENCE AND MARKET SQUARE

CHAPTER 2

MODERN PROVIDENCE AND EXCHANGE PLACE

Exchange Place and the land it is on was once a muddy marsh and could not sustain a large business expansion. But in 1846, with the approval of the Providence City Council, the Providence Worcester Railroad was given permission to develop the area for a railroad system. This modernization allowed the expansion of Exchange Place and modern Downtown Providence, now Kennedy Plaza. (Author's collection.)

The Industrial Trust Building was constructed in 1928 and is a 26-story skyscraper that stands in the heart of Downtown Providence. It is an iconic landmark in New England, and epitomized the rapid economic growth in the region in 1928 among other large retail shopping outlets, retail banking, and professional office buildings. Currently, the building is vacant. (Both, author's collection.)

INDUSTRIAL TRUST BUILDING. PROVIDENCE. RHODE ISLAND

THE PROVIDENCE-BILTMORE HOTEL. PROVIDENCE. R. I.

The Biltmore Hotel, erected in 1922, is on Dorrance Street neighboring Providence City Hall at the western end of Exchange Place. The hotel was a short walk from Union Station, where many visitors stayed overnight in luxury to shop and conduct personal and commercial business downtown. The Biltmore continues as a hotel today as it was in the early days of the city's expansion. (Both, author's collection.)

City Hall and Washington Street,
   Providence, R. I.

P-24539

Providence City Hall was built on Dorrance Street overlooking Exchange Place and is the center of city government. This magnificent building of sculpted stone and iron was dedicated in 1878 by popular Mayor Thomas A. Doyle. The hall was considered expensive to build at $1 million but was necessary to keep up with the downtown's unprecedented economic expansion. Today, this building is still being used as Providence City Hall. (Both, author's collection.)

This postcard from 1913 shows a family with baggage in hand most likely disembarking from Union Station. Many visitors found downtown to be a fascinating place to visit and stay for days or even weeks. Travelers from around the region saw the downtown skyline, city park, and beautiful monuments as they arrived. Today, the city has become a tourist destination for its fine restaurants, colleges and universities, and wonderfully preserved architecture. (Both, author's collection.)

"Skyscrapers" and Banjotti Memorial Fountain from Depot Park, Providence, R. I.

Exchange Street, on the eastern side of Exchange Place Mall, was designed in 1848 and is considered part of the financial district in Downtown Providence. Shown in this image, this area was referred to as "Little Wall Street," denoting its similarity to the larger one in New York City. This group of buildings included banks and financial services. (Both, author's collection.)

EXCHANGE ST., "LITTLE WALL STREET", PROVIDENCE, R. I.

MODERN PROVIDENCE AND EXCHANGE PLACE

Burnside Park was named after Ambrose Burnside, a general in the Civil War. In 1887, Providence erected a monument dedicated to him in front of Union Station. In addition to being a noted general, Burnside was a successful businessman. He owned and managed the Burnside Rifle Works, which became the Rhode Island Locomotive Works in 1865–1866 after the war. This park still exists in Kennedy Plaza. (Both, author's collection.)

MODERN PROVIDENCE AND EXCHANGE PLACE

EXCHANGE PLACE. PROVIDENCE. R. I.

The Exchange Place Mall "Loop" was constructed in the center of Exchange Place because city planners saw the need to centralize an area for the growing visitor traffic to enter and exit the many trolley cars in a safe manner. Also constructed in this area was a pedestrian comfort station in 1914 where passengers could wait in an area protected from weather. This was part of a city-wide plan to make the city more accessible and safer for the commuting public. (Both, author's collection.)

MODERN PROVIDENCE AND EXCHANGE PLACE

The Federal Building was constructed in 1908 at the eastern part of Exchange Place. This building was established after the City of Providence gifted the land to the US government, and contained the post office, federal court, and the custom house. Today, it is still used as a courthouse. (Both, author's collection.)

POST OFFICE PROVIDENCE, R. I.

Union Station, built in 1896 at the north end of Exchange Place, overlooks Burnside Park. This beautiful train station was one significant element that ushered in the new wave of economic expansion of Downtown Providence. The ease for the commuter to visit from around New England allowed for many opportunities to shop and conduct business. Today, this building is occupied by the Rhode Island Foundation. (Both, author's collection.)

Union Depot, Providence, R. I.

60-47

MODERN PROVIDENCE AND EXCHANGE PLACE

The Carrie Brown Bajnotti Memorial Fountain was dedicated in 1902 to the City of Providence by Paul Bajnotti, her husband. This magnificent sculpture was designed by the great sculptor Enid Yandell. The memorial stands elegantly within Kennedy Plaza's Burnside Park. This area of Exchange Place has an inviting garden with ample areas to walk or sit. (Both, author's collection.)

Exchange Place, Showing City Hall,
    Providence, R. I.

Exchange Place was built in 1848. This image looking west from Exchange Street shows the Butler Exchange on the left and the Providence City Hall and a small pedestrian parklike area in the center, which includes the Soldiers and Sailors Monument. The Butler Exchange was demolished and replaced by the Industrial Trust Building in 1928. On the right below is the Biltmore Hotel. (Both, author's collection.)

This postcard of Exchange Place in 1905 displays several moderately sized buildings, except for the Industrial Trust Building in the center and the Banigan Building in the distance on Weybosset Street. The old Industrial Trust Building at far left is gone, as are many of the four- and five-story buildings. This entire area shows how dramatic change can be over a century. (Both, author's collection.)

Depot Park was located at Exchange Place and was the first view of downtown commuters saw when they exited Union Station. This view of the city's skyline around 1928 displays, from left to right, the Turks Head Building, Industrial Trust Building, and Providence City Hall. This area was also called Exchange Place Mall. (Both, author's collection.)

16:—INDUSTRIAL TRUST CO. BLDG. AND DEPOT PARK, PROVIDENCE, R. I.

This postcard shows Exchange Place from Fulton and Exchange Streets; on the left is the majestic Biltmore Hotel, and on the right is Union Station. This mall area has changed several times over the years, and so has the skyline. Today, the area is known as Kennedy Plaza, dedicated in 1964 to the memory of the late Pres. John F. Kennedy. (Both, author's collection.)

The Soldiers and Sailors Monument dedicated in 1871 was built in front of Providence City Hall in honor of the soldiers and sailors from Rhode Island who served in the Civil War. The monument was in Exchange Place because it was the main area for civic gatherings. During the Civil War, Rhode Island was a major supplier to the Union army. (Both, author's collection.)

Looking south on Francis Street, the street that entered Exchange Place via tunnels under Union Station can be seen. This postcard also shows a railroad viaduct over Francis Street to allow for rapid inbound and outbound train traffic. This road was one of the main transportation arteries in the city's new travel strategy implemented in 1889 to alleviate traffic congestion in the city. (Both, author's collection.)

VIEW FROM FRANCIS STREET, PROVIDENCE, R. I.

This southeast view of Exchange Place shows numerous taxis waiting for the many visitors to the city in 1900. Another major mode of transportation used downtown was the trolley car. Taxi and trolley service was made easier for the visitor because one could buy a ticket inside Union Station and then present it outside. All systems of transportation were methodically maintained by the city government by modernizing the city's roads. (Both, author's collection.)

EXCHANGE PLACE, PROVIDENCE, R. I.

1480

MODERN PROVIDENCE AND EXCHANGE PLACE

CHAPTER

CITY VIEWS OF THE DOWNTOWN

WEYBOSSET ST., PROVIDENCE, R. I.

With the expansion of Downtown Providence and the influx of a growing population, the city developed into a thriving metropolitan area that became a magnet for investments and tourism. This image shows an easterly view of Weybosset Street in approximately 1928. This area was an enormous success in the retail marketplace because many of the businesses used a department store strategy of convenience, having all consumer goods under one roof. (Author's collection.)

Weybosset Street, Providence, R. I.

Weybosset Street is one of the most famous streets in Providence and was originally used by the Pequots, the indigenous people of the Narragansett area prior to European settlement. This fabulous street is one of the city's most interesting areas where many people would conduct business, shop, and meet friends and family. It had a variety of popular stores where visitors from all over the northeast visited via taxi, train, and trolley. (Both, author's collection.)

CITY VIEWS OF THE DOWNTOWN

Dorrance Street is one of the busiest streets downtown because it includes several prominent buildings, such as city hall, the Union Trust Building, the Biltmore Hotel, and the Woolworth Building. It was named after the distinguished Judge John Dorrance. In 1886, this cobblestone road was modernized with granite pavers over a concrete base to handle the increased vehicle and pedestrian traffic. (Both, author's collection.)

The Lowes Building, constructed in 1928 on Weybosset Street, is shown on the right and was used as a theater and today is the Providence Performing Arts Center. The tall structure on the left is the Industrial Trust Building, and in the center is the Turks Head Building. This image reveals how Providence's downtown has evolved into a modern city with the old buildings of the past beside the new buildings of the present. (Both, author's collection.)

CITY VIEWS OF THE DOWNTOWN

6992. VIEW FROM PROSPECT TERRACE, PROVIDENCE, R. I.

This view from Prospect Terrace, created in 1867, displays the Downtown Providence skyline. At far left is the Banigan Building, in the center is Providence City Hall, and at far right is Union Station. This vantage point looking down at Exchange Place shows how the skyline has changed in over a century. This beautiful terrace area is now Roger Williams Memorial Park. (Both, author's collection.)

Noon-day Shopping Crowd on Westminster St., Providence, R. I.

Looking east down Westminster Street shows a very busy shopping scene. Many of the high-end retail outlets were on this historic thoroughfare in Downtown Providence. Since 1893, Westminster Street ran from Market Square in the east to Cathedral Square in the west. Besides office buildings and retail stores, there were many restaurants, grocery stores, and cafes. (Both, author's collection.)

CITY VIEWS OF THE DOWNTOWN

This view of Mathewson Street looking north shows horse-drawn wagons and carriages filled with products and pedestrians; this was one of many busy sections of the downtown at this time. On the right is the famous jewelry store Tilden-Thurber, and just beyond it is Gladding's department store. Further down Mathewson Street on the left, past the Berkshire Hotel, was the Lederer Building, erected in 1897, another significant retail and office building. (Both, author's collection.)

Mathewson Street, looking North, Providence. R. I.

This Weybosset Street view of the Arcade, built in 1828, shows a horse-drawn cart and delivery men standing on the granite sidewalk. Inside, people shop and browse the boutiques. This retail outlet extends through to Westminster Street. This entrance is unlike the entrance on Westminster Street. This fine retail structure was one of the first buildings to be erected west of Market Square. (Both, author's collection.)

This view of Westminster Street looking east from Clemence Street shows several businesses in the heart of the retail district of Downtown Providence. Dimond's Department Store, the next tallest building from the left, was a direct competitor with the Outlet Company Store, and at far right is the Train Building, erected in 1893 for an investment property to be rented out as retail space. (Both, author's collection.)

Weybosset Street, Providence, R. I.

Weybosset Street was another popular shopping area downtown and ran parallel to Westminster Street. These two roads were very much the same because both had numerous shopping stores with a variety of goods available for the consumer.

In 1900, there was fierce competition between Shepard's Department Store on Westminster Street and the Outlet Company Store on Weybosset Street. (Both, author's collection.)

This view of Westminster Street looking west shows how vibrant Downtown Providence was in 1910. Along this stretch of road, many pedestrians used electric trolleys and horse-drawn carriages and walked to stores like Hall & Lyon Company, Dimond Company, Boston Store, Shepard's, Cherry and Webb, Gladding's, and Tilden-Thurber, to name a few. These buildings are still used today as retail stores, professional offices, and residential lofts. (Both, author's collection.)

6994. WESTMINSTER STREET, PROVIDENCE, R. I.

This view of Weybosset Street looking west shows many retail shops that were like the ones on Westminster Street in the 1920s. These stores and businesses were found starting from the corner of Dorrance and Mathewson Streets. Some of the businesses on this street included Narragansett Hotel, Outlet Company Store, Lowes Theatre, and Fosters Jewelers. Today, this street is used for small retail outlets, Johnson and Wales University, and Providence Performing Arts Center. (Both, author's collection.)

A914 - Looking up Weybosset St., Providence, R. I.

This image of Westminster Street looking east toward Market Square shows the Arcade, a Greek Revival–style building, and several other storefronts before the new Turks Head Building was built in 1913. The Arcade consisted of three floors with a total of 26 stores on each. The magnificent building has a beautiful glass-covered roof, allowing natural light to illuminate the stores below. (Both, author's collection.)

Weybosset Street is one of the historic roads in Downtown Providence, and at its far eastern end, it connects with Westminster Street to form a major part of Providence's financial district. On this street, the first skyscraper was built in 1896 by Joseph Banigan, shown on the right. On the left is the old Industrial Trust Building, now gone. This historic area still has a significant number of successful restaurants, banks, and office buildings, including the Turks Head Building. (Both, author's collection.)

Industrial Trust Co. and Banigan Building. Providence, R. I.

This view looking east on Westminster Street shows the interesting Turks Head Building's split-V design, where the right side of the structure sits at the corner of Weybosset Street. In the foreground at right is the Union Trust Building, which anchors the Dorrance Street side of Westminster Street. In the middle stands the Lauderdale Building, erected in 1894 as an investment property for the Butler-Duncan Land Company. (Both, author's collection.)

Westminster Street showing Union Trust & Turks

Many of the popular retail stores were on
Westminster Street. This view looking west
shows Dimond's Department Store on the left,
considered Rhode Island's fastest growing store
in 1906. This retail outlet was very popular
because it had numerous products such as
clothing, linens, lamps, hats, and other items
found in current-day shopping malls. (Both,
author's collection.)

WESTMINSTER STREET LOOKING SOUTH, PROVIDENCE R. I.

CITY VIEWS OF THE DOWNTOWN

4

Downtown Providence Retail Buildings

Westminster Street, looking East, Providence, R. J.

This image shows a busy downtown retail district in the middle part of Westminster Street, looking east from Dorrance Street. The large ornate building at left center is the Butler Exchange. This building was demolished for the colossal Industrial Trust Building erected in 1928. The Butler Exchange was a popular retail store in 1873. Also in this image are different modes of transportation that were key to the success of downtown retail businesses. (Both, author's collection.)

The Arcade, built in 1828, is one of the most iconic retail shopping venues in Downtown Providence. It was designed by James Bucklin and Russell Warren and has two distinct entrances; this image shows the one on Westminster Street. The Arcade had food vendors, art galleries, and specialty craft studios for professional photographers and boutique clothing designers. Today, the Arcade continues as the oldest indoor mall in the nation. (Both, author's collection.)

The Boston Store, founded in 1866, was Providence's first department store. The department store concept was a new way of shopping. The Boston Store flourished due to an economic expansion and influx of immigrants from Europe. This influx of people to Providence and New England multiplied the need for larger quantities of consumer goods. Currently, this building is used for upscale loft-style apartments. (Both, author's collection.)

Boston Store, Providence, R. I.

Shepard's Department Store, shown on the left, was founded in 1880 on Westminster Street. By 1903, Shepard's became the largest department store in New England and eventually occupied one city block. Shepard's offered the consumer many items, from clothing to furniture. Unfortunately, the store went bankrupt in 1974 and was a casualty of the exodus of shoppers to suburban malls. This building is now owned by the State of Rhode Island. (Both, author's collection.)

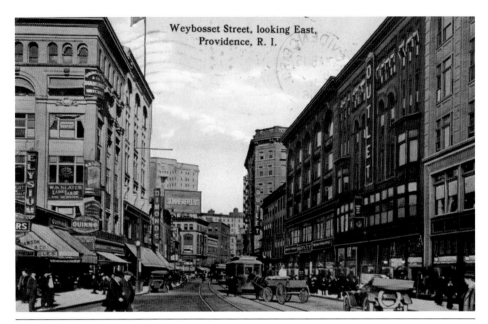

Weybosset Street, looking East, Providence, R. I.

The Outlet Company Store, on the right, was founded in 1891 in the Hodges Building on Weybosset Street. This department store became so successful, it expanded to an entire city block. The Outlet Company Store competed directly with the more established stores, such as Shepard's, Gladding's, and the Boston Store. The building was destroyed by fire in 1986, and the vacant land was purchased by Johnson and Wales University. (Both, author's collection.)

Corner of Westminster and Mathewson Sts. showing Lapham Building, Providence, R. I.

Tilden-Thurber was established on Westminster Street in 1895. This upscale jewelry store, seen on the right, had a reputation for selling fine jewelry and elegant silverware. Many of these stores had large display windows to entice the curious public to peer in and window shop from the street. Today, this building is used for retail space. (Both, author's collection.)

DOWNTOWN PROVIDENCE RETAIL BUILDINGS

The Cherry and Webb Store, seen left of center in this postcard, was a popular department store established on Westminster Street in 1914 and focused on women's apparel. As the store grew, it purchased radio station WPRO in 1935. Unfortunately, the store closed in 1979 because consumers were leaving for the convenience of suburban shopping centers. (Both, author's collection.)

Gladding's, shown at far left, was at the intersection of Westminster and Mathewson Streets. This store was established in 1805, and moved to the larger Burrill Building in 1891 because of the economic expansion in the late 1880s. It was one of the oldest stores in Providence. Gladding's catered to women's fashion. (Both, author's collection.)

The Woolworth Building, built in 1922, replaced the Dorrance Hotel on the corner of Westminster and Dorrance Streets. This was another large department store that would dominate the affordable merchandise market in this area for many years. These five-and-dime stores were numerous throughout the United States during this time. The Woolworth Building is now occupied by a bank. (Both, author's collection.)

Westminster Street had numerous retail businesses, and was the shopping center of the downtown. In this view looking east, at far right is the Union Trust Building, and next to it is the Dorrance Building, constructed in 1876. The Dorrance Building housed Barnaby's dry goods store. This store was significant because it was one of the first retail outlets that established a foothold in the area after the Civil War. (Both, author's collection.)

WESTMINSTER AND EDDY STREETS, PROVIDENCE, R. I.

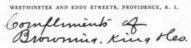

The Arnold Building at the intersection of Washington and Mathewson Streets in Downtown Providence was built in 1896. It was named after its developer, William Arnold, a prominent real-estate developer. On the first floor were retail stores, and on the top floor were offices. William's son George Arnold was also a local businessman and land developer. This building now houses a restaurant. (Both, author's collection.)

Washington & Mathewson Sts.
Providence, R. I.

The Hall & Lyon Company drugstores, established in 1890 in Providence, were considered the largest drugstore in the country at one time. This image shows several retail stores at the intersection of Weybosset and Mathewson Streets, and in the middle is the Hall & Lyon store, with many advertisements on its exterior. Hall & Lyon also had a location in the Providence Journal Building on Westminster Street. (Both, author's collection.)

Weybosset and Mathewson Streets, Providence, R. I.

CHAPTER 5

FINANCIAL AND PROFESSIONAL BUILDINGS

ovidence, R.I., Westminster Street from Union Trust Building

This bird's-eye view overlooks Weybosset Street from the top of the Union Trust Building. In the background is the eastern part of the city near Market Square. In the middle of the postcard are two of the financial district's office buildings: the old Industrial Trust Building on the left, built in 1892, and the Banigan Building on the right, built in 1896. Many of these buildings became symbols of the financial success of the city. (Both, author's collection.)

The Turks Head Building was erected in 1913 at the intersection of Westminster and Weybosset Streets. It was constructed in a time of advanced economic transition and was used for office space for lawyers, stock and bond brokers, and real estate and insurance agents. The building is still used today as office space. (Both, author's collection.)

The Banigan Building was constructed in 1896 by Joseph Banigan in the center of Providence's financial district at 10 Weybosset Street. This was the first city skyscraper at 10 stories high. The building was used for office space. In 1955, it became the offices of Amica Insurance Company and was renamed for that company. It continues as offices for the insurance company today. (Both, author's collection.)

The Union Trust Building was erected in 1901 at the intersection of Dorrance and Westminster Streets by Marsden J. Perry. This magnificent 12-story building was the headquarters of the Union Trust Company, with a bank on the first floor. Today, this historic building is an upscale apartment complex and has an elegant restaurant on the first floor. (Both, author's collection.)

10691   UNION TRUST BUILDING, PROVIDENCE, R. I.

The Hospital Trust Building was erected in 1917 and was originally created to finance Rhode Island Hospital. It was designed in a U-shape and was the first trust company in New England. Hospital Trust was built in the historic Market Square area. It became one of the area's most successful businesses. The building is currently owned by RISD. (Both, author's collection.)

FINANCIAL AND PROFESSIONAL BUILDINGS

The Providence Journal Building, constructed in 1906, was the head office of the *Providence Journal*, the largest newspaper publisher in Rhode Island. The major enterprise outgrew this building and moved in 1934. One of the most distinct structures on Westminster Street, it was used by a variety of retailers. Today, it is vacant. (Both, author's collection.)

The Equitable Building, third from left, was built in 1872. In the center sits the Wilcox Building, erected in 1875. And on its right is the Bank of North America Building, constructed in 1856. These medium-size office buildings on Weybosset Street catered to the commercial and retail public's financial service needs. These three buildings are clustered together in the financial district of Downtown Providence. (Both, author's collection.)

The Exchange Bank was built in 1888 on the corner of Exchange and Westminster Streets across from the Turks Head Building. Exchange Bank is four and a half stories high and is minuscule compared to the other enormous buildings it is surrounded by in Downtown Providence. This building was used for banking and office space and is used today as retail space. (Past, courtesy of Providence Public Library. Identifier: VM011_03_03_166. This image was cropped and sharpened for publication; present, author's collection.)

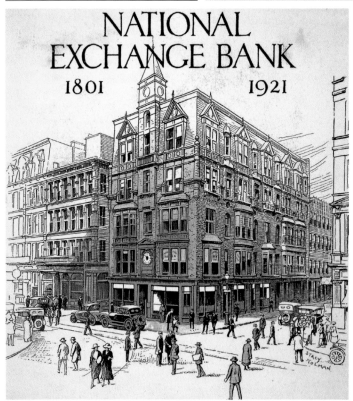

NATIONAL EXCHANGE BANK
1801   1921

FINANCIAL AND PROFESSIONAL BUILDINGS

Merchant Bank, erected in 1857 and seen here at center, is at the eastern edge of Westminster Street and is a small-statured building at only six stories high. This bank was established before the great surge in business activity in Downtown Providence. Merchant Bank was used for retail banking and office space and is nicely located in the financial district. In 1920, the bank became part of Providence National Bank. (Both, author's collection.)

Providence Institute for Savings, also known as Old Stone Bank, was established in 1819, and in 1854 constructed a small branch office on South Main Street. Although a modest building, it became iconic after the owners undertook a very ornate remodeling in 1898. This was one of the business buildings in the downtown that illustrates the fascinating economic boom time of Providence. Today, the bank is closed, and the building is vacant. (Both, author's collection.)

CHAPTER 6

BUILDINGS GONE
FROM THE PAST

RHODE ISLAND COLLEGE OF EDUCATION, PROVIDENCE, R. I.   18568

The Rhode Island College of Education, built in 1898, was originally called the Normal School. This higher learning institution was near the state capitol building, and its main function was to train teachers for Rhode Island's public schools. The institute later became Rhode Island College in 1959 and moved to a larger campus in the Mount Pleasant area of Providence. Today, this building has been replaced by the Providence Place Mall. (Author's collection.)

83

The Crown Hotel was built in 1894 on Weybosset Street next to the Outlet Company Store. The Crown was a convenient place to stay because it was centrally located within walking distance of the major areas of interest, and only charged $1.50 per night for a room. In 1950, Johnson and Wales University purchased the Crown Hotel for dormitories. In 1992, the building was demolished due to its age. (Both, author's collection.)

Narragansett Hotel,
Providence, R. I.

The Narragansett Hotel, erected in 1878 on Weybosset Street, was a beautiful eight-story building with 225 exquisitely designed rooms that overlooked the city. This hotel was designed by a select group of wealthy Providence investors that included the great Nelson Aldrich. It had lavish dining rooms, barbershops, and other areas to shop and lounge. The hotel was demolished in 1960. (Both, author's collection.)

The old Industrial Trust Building was erected in 1892 at the intersection of Westminster and Exchange Streets and was one of the banks in the financial district of Downtown Providence. In 1928, the bank moved its offices to the new Industrial Trust Building skyscraper at 111 Westminster Street. Unfortunately, the old Industrial Trust Building was demolished in 1970. Now, this location is occupied by Santander Bank. (Both, author's collection.)

The old Union Station was constructed by the Providence & Worcester Railroad in 1848 in the center of Exchange Place but was destroyed by fire in 1896. The new Union Station was built farther north to relieve the area's traffic congestion. The new, larger Union Station was needed for a more efficient flow of traffic because of the large influx of visitors from throughout New England. (Both, author's collection.)

D UNION STATION, PROVIDENCE, R. I.

The Dorrance Hotel was built in 1880 on the corner of Westminster and Dorrance Streets. It was a popular place to stay because it was in a great area where one could find world-class shopping and many financial institutions to conduct business. This fine hotel was eventually torn down to make way for the Woolworth Building in 1920. (Both, author's collection.)

The Butler Exchange, located at Exchange Place, was founded in 1873. This building was used by the Providence Telephone Company in 1879. Developed by Cyrus Butler to be used as office space and for retail businesses, this well-designed building was later demolished to make way for the Industrial Trust Building in 1928. (Both, author's collection.)

Infantry Hall, showing So. Main St., Providence. R. I.

Infantry Hall was built in 1879–1880 on South Main Street by the First Light Infantry Regiment of Rhode Island. This was the city's main theater, with seating for 2,000. The space was used for a multitude of events, such as live musicals and political gatherings. One notable act that performed there was the Boston Symphony Orchestra. Unfortunately, Infantry Hall was demolished in 1952. (Both, author's collection.)

BUILDINGS GONE FROM THE PAST

This view of Weybosset Street looking east shows a very busy shopping zone in 1900. Many of these shops had cloth awnings on their first floors to shade the pedestrian window shoppers. The expansion on this side of the city was dominated by the Outlet Company Store. Among the buildings that were bought out and demolished by the Outlet Company was Wirth's Café, shown at far right. (Both, author's collection.)

Keith's New Theatre on Westminster Street was rededicated in 1912. This theater had several name changes over the years. Prior to 1912, it was known as the Lows Opera House, and in 1919, it was called the Victory Theatre; in 1935, it was the Empire Theatre. The theater was very popular because of its interesting shows. In 1949, the building was demolished due to its age. (Both, author's collection.)

CORNER OF DORRANCE AND WEYBOSSET STREET, HOWING THE NARRAGANSETT HOTEL, PROVIDENCE, R. I.

Looking down Dorrance Street at its intersection with Weybosset Street shows the Narragansett Hotel, and just beyond it to the left, the Providence Opera House, built in 1871. The opera house was a great entertainment venue of the time and showed plays, operas, and musicals. The building was eventually demolished in 1931 to expand the more-successful Outlet Company Store. (Both, author's collection.)

City Hotel, one of the old landmarks on Weybosset Street, Providence, R. I.

The City Hotel, built in 1832 on Weybosset Street, was a famous hotel for many visiting dignitaries to Rhode Island. The hotel was visited by many US presidents, most notably Abraham Lincoln. Due to a rapid expansion of the Outlet Company Store, it and many other older buildings in the area were torn down. (Both, author's collection.)

BUILDINGS GONE FROM THE PAST

BIBLIOGRAPHY

Barker, Henry Ames. *Providence: A Reference Book & Guide to a City of Varied Fascinations*. Providence Standard Printing Co., 1910.

Cady, John Hutchins. *The Civic and Architectural Development of Providence: 1636–1950*. Providence, RI: The Book Shop, 1957.

Conley, Patrick T., and Paul R. Campbell. *Providence: A Pictorial History*. Virginia Beach, VA: Donning Company, 1982.

Jordy, William H. *Buildings of Rhode Island*. New York, NY: Oxford University Press, 2004.

Providence Journal, The. *Rhode Island Memories: The Early Years*. Battle Ground, WA: Pediment Publishing, 2018.

Rhode Island Historical Society Research Department reference materials.

Smart, Samuel Chipman. *The Outlet Story: 1894–1984*. Providence, RI: Outlet Communications, 1984.

Woodward, William McKenzie. *Downtown Providence*. Providence, RI: Rhode Island Historical Preservation Commission, 1981.

——————. *Guide to Providence Architecture*. Providence, RI: Providence Preservation Society, 2003.

——————. *Providence: A Citywide Survey of Historic Resources*. Providence, RI: Rhode Island Historical Preservation Commission, 1986.

DISCOVER THOUSANDS OF LOCAL HISTORY BOOKS FEATURING MILLIONS OF VINTAGE IMAGES

Arcadia Publishing, the leading local history publisher in the United States, is committed to making history accessible and meaningful through publishing books that celebrate and preserve the heritage of America's people and places.

Find more books like this at
www.arcadiapublishing.com

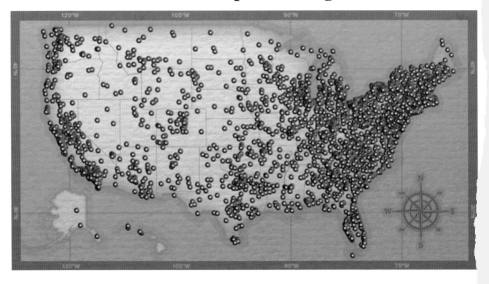

Search for your hometown history, your old stomping grounds, and even your favorite sports team.

Consistent with our mission to preserve history on a local level, this book was printed in South Carolina on American-made paper and manufactured entirely in the United States. Products carrying the accredited Forest Stewardship Council (FSC) label are printed on 100 percent FSC-certified paper.